Momentary Infinity

Dylan Oxley

Copyright © Dylan Oxley, 2025

This book is copyright. Apart from any fair dealing for the purposes of study and research, criticism, review, or as otherwise permitted under the Copyright Act, no part may be reproduced by any process without written permission. Inquiries should be made to the publisher.

Independently published by Dylan Oxley.

Cover design by Patrick Girouard.

Contents

1	Momentary Infinity
2	Beauty Burns
3	A Third of a Life
4	Duality
5	Same Hands
6	Fool's Gold
7	Comfy Cage
8	Holding Pattern
9	Taste Test
10	The More You Know
11	10 Steps to a Better Life
12	Zombies and Robots
13	Bittersweet Relief
14	Living Dead
15	Are You Alive Yet?
16	The Dying Room
17	Just Keep Counting
18	Funeral Home
19	Resumés
20	Flowers
21	Grieve Greedily
22	You Haven't Lived

23	Hurry Home
24	Simple Man
25	Draw
26	Eyes for You
27	Loveletting
28	The Contract
30	Please Read Carefully Before Use
31	Your Ghosts
32	Falling Forever
33	Somebody
34	Thinking of You
35	Happiness Attack
36	Universe in Me
37	Setting Son
38	Discrepancy
39	HAPPINESS?
40	Silence
41	A Beautiful Mess
42	Truce
43	Warcry
44	March
45	Alchemy
46	Coup de Grâce
47	Write

48	Apologies for the Inconvenience
49	Kindness
50	Retail Therapist
51	Join the Club
52	Cannibals
54	Volumes
55	The Space Between Breaths
56	Almost Alive
57	(Ad)vice
58	Neighbours
59	Greetings
60	To the Person in Front of Me
61	Sometimes
63	The Best Things in Life are Free*
64	Holy Hell
65	Catch and Release
66	Secrets
67	Sparrows
68	The Music of Nature
69	Phantom Limbs
70	Doorway
71	Grow Down
73	Speed Signs
74	Jigsaw

75	The Price I Pay
77	Clock Face
78	Broken Vases
79	Cold Coffee
80	Benefit of the Doubt
81	Life Lessons
82	Impatient
83	No Loss
84	Metamorphosis
85	Oracles
86	About the Author

For my grandmothers, Lois and Lynette.

Momentary Infinity

From existence to extinction
a dream to a memory
we are all supernovas shining
from lightyears away.

You are a pinprick
in a black blanket
draped over a spinning globe
as the moon reminds us
there is light on the other side
while we sleep in darkness.

But I see you.

I am a shooting star
burning bright
a beautiful death
in broad daylight
with nobody to make
a wish upon me.

Do you see me too?

Beauty Burns

I'm still trying to find
my place in the world
where others live in ignorance
of their brilliance.

I may die
searching the sky for
a light like my own
from the forest floor
buried in brightness.

The dead stars are
beautiful in their burning
but even they all look the same
this far away.

My greatest fear
is being forgotten
but even I don't know
who I am yet.

A Third of a Life

If I spend
a third of my life working
and a third sleeping
I only get a third
to live to the fullest.

But if I can do
what I love for a living
and dream about the day
maybe I can be whole
for a little while.

Duality

I struggle with the duality
of seeing light and dark
in each moment
and trying to figure out
which one feels right.

Like when you put your hand
under running water
and your brain takes a second
to discern if it's freezing cold
or boiling hot.

Perhaps everything is
a bit of both.

Same Hands

I read my palms

creased and calloused

and marvel at how

these are the same hands

that put pen to paper

and finger to key

as a form of penance for

the crimes they have committed.

Fool's Gold

Sometimes
you have to settle
for a subtle substitute
while you wait for
the real thing.

Sometimes
a heart of pyrite
or storm clouds with
a stainless steel lining
will have to do.

At least you won't
feel so heavy
and the bright blue sky
won't rust from the rain.

Comfy Cage

My bedroom has become
a comfy cage
as I watch the birds fly
outside my window.

The recycled air
and artificial light
are the only elements
in my world of one.

I could walk through the door
and join them in the yard
but I can only admire
their freedom from the ground.

So this is how it feels
to be one of those animals
living behind glass walls
I pay money to get close to.

Holding Pattern

Life can feel like
you're stuck in a holding pattern
stopping to refuel every now and then
with a holiday here and there
but never really going anywhere.

So if you're going to
keep flying in circles
at least make a point
of looking out the window
and talking to the person beside you.

Taste Test

When I pass strangers in the street
I often wonder what it would be like
to live in their world for a little while.

Who are they today?
Where are they going?
What are they thinking?

Do they have a purpose?
Do they have a dream?
Do they have a secret?

Just a taste test of another life
before I get back to my own
bland existence.

The More You Know

If I could give
my younger self
one piece of advice
it would be to fail
as much as possible.

The more you try
the more you know
and the more you know
the more you try.

Now that I'm older
my only regret is
I didn't try hard enough
and I still don't know anything.

10 Steps to a Better Life

1. Throw your mobile phone into the ocean as a digital message in a bottle.
2. Drive home from work in reverse to feel like you're getting the time back.
3. Walk to the shops in your pyjamas so you can say you're buying dreams.
4. Swap background music for birdsong and speaking for listening.
5. Give your cat double the serving suggestion at least once a week.
6. Watch your favourite movie with a stranger and ask them for theirs.
7. Call that friend you haven't seen for years to tell them you love them.
8. Write your name on a piece of paper and burn it to start from scratch.
9. Listen to the trees in the wind and whisper back an honest answer.
10. Sleep outside on the grass under the stars for a new perspective on life.

Zombies and Robots

I imagine a future
overrun by zombies
and robots.

The undead and
the unconscious
shambling around
or zipping about
with no concept of time
or love or death.

I hope I never live
to see the day
I find my people
in a funeral home
or a hardware store.

Bittersweet Relief

Like the kiss
of a hundred needles
I repeat the point
until I no longer feel it.

But like the blanket
of dust on a skeleton
the knowledge of my death
will not comfort me.

Living Dead

Sometimes
I get so afraid to live
I feel like a wandering ghost.

The fragility of life
leaves me frozen in fear
like a car I'm afraid to drive
in case I scratch it.

Because if I go somewhere
and do something
with somebody
I could die someday.

I've mourned the life I never had
and ignored the one I do.

But I'd rather go to my grave
with beauty scars and smile lines
than wish lists and dead dreams.

Are You Alive Yet?

The leading cause of death
in people over the age of thirty
is anonymity.

Social suicide rates
are through the roof
of our mouths shut tight
around the hand that feeds
our screens with slop.

You barely survive your twenties
making a name for yourself
to replace the one given to you.

Then all of a sudden
you look more like your shadow
than your reflection
in the cold light of day.

A faceless ghost
haunting the dreams
of your former self.

The Dying Room

If the room with the TV
where we escape reality
with open eyes
is called the living room
then the room with the bed
where we close them
to embrace fantasy
should be called the dying room.

A place where
dreams are stillborn
and innocence draws
its final breath.

We all resign from the day
in a thousand-thread count shroud
on a mattress moulded
by the weight of waking life
to rest our heavy heads
and sleep away the loneliness.

Just Keep Counting

Dying sounds like something
that happens to other people.

My brain refuses to believe
my body will betray it someday
yet knowing this
beautifully pointless life
could end at any moment
makes it all worth it.

So revel in the small joys
of sunrises and meteors
and payday and coffee
and laughing until you cry.

I'm not running
and I'm not hiding
but I'm not standing around
just waiting for it either.

Ready or not
here it comes.

Funeral Home

I live near a funeral home
and check the chimney for smoke
every time I drive past.

One day
I think
that will be me.

A wisp in the wind
amongst the crows
and exhaust fumes.

But until then
I follow the road.

Resumés

Resumés are like
practise obituaries
but the irony is
we never write our own
in the end.

I'll be your reference
if you'll be mine.

Flowers

I used to wonder why
we give flowers to those
who are grieving.

Something sweet
that will surely die
as they mourn a loss.

Now I see
there is beauty in brevity
and the wilting petals
are a gentle reminder
nothing we love can stay.

Grieve Greedily

When I'm gone
don't feel bad for me
but don't feel bad for yourself either.

Crack a joke at my funeral
go out on my birthday
and turn my bedroom into a studio.

I'll forgive you for forgetting me
by filling the space where I was
with things that make you happy.

You Haven't Lived

You haven't lived until you've wept at a poem.
You haven't lived until you've laughed at yourself.
You haven't lived until you've quit a job.
You haven't lived until you've fallen in love.
You haven't lived until you've played with a child.
You haven't lived until you've conversed with a bird.
You haven't lived until you've written a letter to the world.
You haven't lived until you've died.

Hurry Home

Everybody else is in a hurry
to get home and do nothing
while I drive around for hours
when I've got somewhere to be.

Would you like to
take the scenic route
to the cemetery
with me?

Simple Man

200,000 years
of human evolution
and all I can think about
is food
        and sex
                and death.

Draw

We kept fighting
when we had nothing
left to fight for
but I would still
rather raise a red flag
than wave a white one.

I let you in
and let you win
but now I'm out
it's your loss.

Love is a
victory speech
for an epitaph.

Eyes for You

If love is blind
then heartfelt hate
is such a sorry sight.

You could never
see before me
but I'll always
look after you.

Loveletting

Exhumed heartache
curdles grief into bitterness
like an autopsy of the self
with a sharp tongue under blue light.

Bleed the hurt out
before it metastasises
and travels to the heart
then kills you all over again.

The Contract

This is a formal agreement to the terms and conditions of engaging in emotional relations (the Contract) between you (the End User) and the issuer of this statement (the Body).

Please read carefully and agree to the below before proceeding:

- The End User will provide adequate physical affection and sufficient emotional support in a timely manner.
- The End User will be available for all business proposals including, but not limited to: private events, public outings, social gatherings, and living arrangements.
- The Body reserves the right to reprimand the End User for any misconduct in whichever way they deem fit.
- The End User accepts full responsibility of any and all possible outcomes.
- The End User will not release any defamatory information should a breach of the Contract occur.

- The Contract may be terminated at any time by the Body for any reason.
- The Body cannot be held liable for any damages caused by a breach of the Contract.

If the End User agrees to enter into the Contract with the Body, please sign and date the following statement.

I, _____, hereby consent to engage in emotional relations with the Body as of __/__/____. I have read and understand the above terms and conditions and will uphold these values to the best of my ability.*

* Terms and conditions subject to change without prior notice.

Please Read Carefully Before Use

WARNING!

Proceed with caution

Watch your step

Slippery when wet

Press and hold to release

Do not leave unattended

Ensure your own safety before assisting others

Keep out of reach of children

Do not accept if seal is broken

Void if damaged

Avoid contact with eyes

If irritation occurs stop using immediately

If symptoms persist consult your doctor

Please dispose of responsibly

Your Ghosts

You are haunted by your past
and you keep your ghosts
on a short leash so you can
pull them into the light
to scare off the living dead.

Let them go
and take my hand instead.

Falling Forever

I steal glances at a girl's eyes
like she has suns in her sockets
but to them I am nothing more
than another smiling name
fumbling through his thanks
who they will forget
by the next in line.

I fall in love
with somebody new
almost every day
and they always
break my heart.

Somebody

Somebody is out there
looking for love
and I am patiently waiting
for them to find me.

Thinking of You

We haven't talked
for a long time
but I want you to know
I think of you often
and wonder if you
think of me too.

So I'll leave this
poem right here
just in case
you still watch me
from afar
wherever you are.

Happiness Attack

Sometimes
a message from a friend
will fill my heart
with so much joy
it overflows into
uncontrollable laughter
like a nervous tic.

When it's my time to go
I hope it's a cardiac arrest
from happiness.

Universe in Me

There will be no empty space
when you leave this world
because you have already left
an entire universe in me
and I see you everywhere.

Setting Son

I will try to spend
the rest of your life
aboveground
so you don't have to
see your only son
set in soil.

Discrepancy

The people who love you
care much more than you think
and the people who don't
care nowhere near as little.

HAPPINESS?

How
Are
People
Pleasers
In
Never
Ending
Sorry
States
?

Silence

The sound of every statue
thinking out loud
is breaking the silence
between my ears
until all I can hear
is the weight of time
crushing me from the inside.

If these walls could talk
I would be out of a job.

A Beautiful Mess

I am a beautiful mess
like tangled Christmas lights
or shredded birthday balloons.

A butterfly on the windscreen
or a smashed jar of jelly beans.

Point and laugh
at all the pretty colours
as I get myself cleaned up.

Truce

Whether one
gives a thumbs up
or the middle finger
I will shake my own hand
because the enemy
       of my enemy
              is my friend.

Always remember
the truth lies within.

When was the last time
you smiled at a mirror?

Warcry

There's something about
dying light
that makes me feel
so alive.

The pretty sight
a small victory
as the sun slips into
its grave for the night
only to be resurrected
the next mourning.

A yawning eulogy
for a warcry
as I prepare for battle
once again.

March

Fall into step
with the rhythm of life.

Left   Right
Left   Right
Stop

Give way to change.

The leaves will dry up
like your happiness
but only for a little while.

Harmonise with the
hum of the highway
make music from
the morning malady
and march on.

It wasn't named after
the god of war
for nothing.

Alchemy

Making art alchemises
the pain into medicine
and makes your private hell
safe for public consumption
so it can live outside of you
instead of dying with you.

It becomes something
you can see
        and hear
                and touch.

Share it with the world
so you don't suffer for nothing
and heal yourself by knowing
it helps other people like you
who carry around their fool's gold
to feel a little lighter.

Coup de Grâce

A hard hit
in a soft spot
hurts like a helping hand
from a forgotten friend.

The right chords
at the wrong time
or a final kiss goodbye.

Killing with kindness
is disservice with a smile
reminding you how to breathe.

Write

Write like you mean it.
Write like you owe the page something.
Write like you never forgave its blankness.
Write like you have to earn the words.

Write like you're hiding from your parents.
Write like you're whispering to your lover.
Write like you're confiding in your best friend.
Write like you're laughing at yourself.

Write like you're leading a protest.
Write like you're waging a war.
Write like you're committing a crime.
Write like you're standing on trial.

Write like your life depends on it.
Because it does.

Apologies for the Inconvenience

My best ideas
always arrive at
the worst times.

When I'm driving.
When I'm eating.
When I'm waiting in line.
When I'm having a shower.
When I'm trying to fall asleep.

I wish they would
at least call ahead
so I can unlock the door
and leave a light on.

Kindness

Working in retail for ten years
has taught me how not to treat
a helpful stranger.

But I've also learned how to be
patient and forgiving
when a person is angry and confused.

You never know
what kind of day somebody is having
so don't take their kindness for granted.

Retail Therapist

Sometimes
I feel like
a retail therapist.

People come into my work
and tell me their problems
to wring some sort of sympathy
out of our ~~transaction~~ interaction.

The best I can do is offer them
a discount on a new one.

Would you like
a copy of your receipt?

Join the Club

Born to work to death
9 to 5 to life

Clock in.
Do time.
Clock out.

Hired
      Tired
            Pre   re   tired
Fired
      Wired
            Un   in   spired

Earn a living.
Spend it dying.

Cannibals

We shuffle through checkouts
with our cash and cards ready
like cattle queueing up for
a bolt between the eyes.

Minced through the turnstile
and spat out by the system
of sorry self-service
selling identity for herd immunity
to wear foreign name brands
as protection from each other
when we all look the same.

The only choice we have
is if we close our eyes
when they shoot
with the tap of a button
just to try again.

You are what you eat
and we can't seem to get
enough of ourselves.

Starving for attention
in a mirror maze of one-way glass
where the only exit is through
the empty eyes of guilty bystanders
that autofocus on your imperfections.

So smile
you are on camera.

Volumes

It is your duty to stand up
for what you believe in.

To break the silence
before you bend a knee.

Keep your spine straight
and your head high
in the face of injustice.

Fight to the death
with words and wit
against every dumb thing.

The Space Between Breaths

I've defused more conflicts
by listening than speaking
and answered more questions
by asking my own.

Strange things happen
in the space between breaths
where a moment to think
can change the world.

Almost Alive

Fitting into polite society
is slow suicide by
a lack of truth to the heart.

That's why speaking from it
is always more honest than
what comes out of your mouth.

But you trick yourself with
scare tactics and reverse psychology
to feed it white lies and small talk
so you don't wince at every word
in a song or film or book.

The truth hurts
because it makes you realise
for just a second
you were almost alive.

So lick your bloody lips
and be prepared to face
the consequences.

(Ad)vice

I can't help but laugh
at the shops and businesses
clustered together
in my hometown.

A doctor next to a tobacconist.
A chemist beside a bottle shop.
A bank across from a tavern.

Advice and vices are
next-door neighbours
where I come from.

Neighbours

I can hear the neighbours
yelling at each other about
how one thinks the other
only thinks about themselves
as I think about them
not thinking about me
from a wall away.

Greetings

I love catching people
                       off-guard
with my greetings.

It's so easy to fall into
our rehearsed responses
that we don't even realise
we aren't paying attention.

We might as well be
talking to ourselves.

"Hey there."
                "Good thanks."
"Not bad."
                "You too."

To the Person in Front of Me

The car in front of me indicates
in the middle of the road
so I start to slow down until
they swerve around another car
I didn't even know was there
and I admire how strangers
save our lives every day.

We are all unsung heroes
to people we have never met
in our own oblivious way.

Sometimes

Sometimes
I wake up
with a song in my head
I haven't heard for years
and remember all the words.

Sometimes
I write my name
and brush my teeth
with my non-dominant hand
as practise for if I lose the other.

Sometimes
I count my steps
and always try to finish
on an even number.

Sometimes
I use a fake name
when I order coffee
just to feel like
somebody else for a day.

Sometimes
I say hello
to homeless people
just in case
nobody else does.

Sometimes
I feel the leaves
of passing trees
as if shaking hands
with an old friend.

The Best Things in Life are Free*

Everything
is trying to sell me
something.

I was driving home from the city
past ads on shops and bus stops
when I saw a burned billboard
with its blackened edges
curled up in a hideous snarl
and I smiled to myself
as I turned my gaze to
the clouds and trees instead.

Holy Hell

Powerlines cut through the sky
between upright limbless corpses
like redacted truths of nature
the birds perch on for
a taste of civilisation
as we worship them from below.

Catch and Release

I try to take a photo
of the bright white moon
through the trees
as the sun rises
but I can't quite get it right
so I'm forced to just enjoy it
with my own two eyes.

A reminder
not everything beautiful
should be captured.

Secrets

There are secrets
hidden in shooting stars
and sunsets.

Go outside
and let the sky show you
what it knows.

Sparrows

I watch three sparrows
dance on the floor of the café
from my table with
a plant in a bottle beside me
this brisk Wednesday morning
like tiny cheerleaders championing
the workers through the week.

Nature lets itself in
to hide from all the noise
of man and machine outside
and I feel at home in this
world between worlds
with coffee and cake.

The Music of Nature

I hear birds in the morning
bugs in the evening
and   people
        TVs
        cars
        planes
        sirens
and   gunshots
all
damn
day.

The music of nature
bookends the noise of life
so I can sleepwalk
through the static.

Phantom Limbs

Tree stumps line the road
like blank tombstones
as phantom limbs
beckon the bereaved
on their way to work
and I can't be sure
if the widowed branches
swaying in the breeze
are waving or drowning.

Doorway

Walking in misty rain
feels like a doorway
to my childhood.

When you're a kid
it's fun to go out and get wet
without a care in the world.

When you're an adult
you do all you can not to
and consider the weather
an inconvenience.

So I close my eyes
hang my head back
as the pins and needles
dance upon my face
and let it transport me
to a simpler time.

Grow Down

We lose the wonder of childhood
to the fear of reality.

The magic of Santa Claus
and the Tooth Fairy
is traded for the rule of gods
and the government.

Curiosity is quashed by certainty
and imaginary friends
become ghosts of our past.

                                    One minute
the topic of conversation
is the colour of flowers.

                                    The next
the price of fuel.

Reclaim your inner child
do what you want
and say what you mean.

Grow d
     o
     w
     n

         grow   s   i   d   e
           w   a   y   s   if you must
but whatever you do
                                         p.
               never grow   u

Speed Signs

One day
you're learning to drive
in an empty carpark
then all of a sudden
you're passing birthdays
like speed signs
and running late to
where you don't want to be.

You figure out how to steer
then engage the cruise control
and spend so much time
looking in the rearview mirror
you forget to watch
where you're going.

Jigsaw

Each year feels like
I've found another
piece of the puzzle.

A reason to live
between the cushions
and a glimmer of hope
behind the fridge.

The less I worry
the more I understand
and begin to see
the bigger picture.

We earn the answers
by making it up
as we go along.

The Price I Pay

Growing up has felt like
a series of small deaths.

I have an identity crisis
each time I look in the mirror.

I lose my hair in the shower
and find it up my nose.

I feel like I've aged
ten years in two
and adopted the habits
of my grandparents
five decades too soon.

I've cracked the code
early in the game
but it comes at the cost
of losing a life overnight
and I've grown
faster than I can grieve
who I used to be.

So I just sit outside
and watch the birds
as crows claw at
the corners of my eyes.

The price I pay
for living life to the fullest
at half-time.

Clock Face

The hands of the clock
sculpt us into ugly things.

Carving lines into our faces.
Wringing the colour from our hair.
Plucking the teeth from our smiles.

But to read the time
with the same old eyes
after all those years
is a beautiful sight.

Broken Vases

Our bodies betray us
bones and all
in due time.

Our minds let us go
to fend for ourselves
in a losing fight.

But the love lingers
the hate dissipates
and beauty abides
by our promises.

Even in decay
we bloom anew
if only on the inside.

Cold Coffee

Sometimes
I go to take a sip of coffee
and when I look down
there's just one mouthful left.

So I wait
to savour the moment
but it's always cold
by the time I finally finish it.

Sometimes
trying to make
good things last
turns them bad.

Benefit of the Doubt

The best decision
will feel like
the worst mistake
until you make it
and realise it was
the only option.

Life Lessons

The hardest tests hold
the greatest lessons in life.

You can't study for them
until you've already failed
and once you have the answers
it's too late to try again.

The student
becomes the teacher
becomes the cleaner
nobody notices.

Sometimes
you have to take
two steps back
to leap forward.

Impatient

When we are young
we are too ignorant to know
wisdom comes with age.

When we are old
we are too impatient to hear
what the innocent see.

No Loss

I have a new rule:
only buy the thing
if you're likely to use it
in the next month
and get rid of it
if you haven't used it
in the last twelve.

So I went through my old stuff
and all I kept were the things
that meant something to me.

The rest went to charity
or family and friends
so it could mean something
to somebody else.

Lose something
every once in a while
and delight in the
perfect meaninglessness
of not knowing where it is.

Metamorphosis

We shed our shells
as we push through the pain
and emerge on the other side
naked but hardened
by the birth of the person
inside of us who
we must die to create.

Oracles

The advice we need
is rarely what we want
to hear so
in a way
we already know the answer.

We are each
our own oracles
we are just
too damn stubborn
to accept it.

What are you keeping
from yourself?

About the Author

Dylan Oxley is an alternative art enthusiast and culture commentator based in Brisbane, Australia. He also makes music as Amity and posts regularly on Substack (*The Drip Tray*). You can follow him on Instagram (@amityvillain) or reach out via email (dylan_amity@hotmail.com) for more strange thoughts and interesting connections.

www.ingramcontent.com/pod-product-compliance
Lightning Source LLC
Chambersburg PA
CBHW022020290426
44109CB00015B/1253